Paper Crafts

This book provides both the techniques and projects to encourage student artists to create works of art using primarily paper, scissors, and glue. Each project provides:

- materials list
- step-by-step directions for specific project
- reproducible patterns where needed
- variations on the project

Table of Contents

Before You Begin

The projects in Paper Crafts are marked by stars to show the levels of difficulty. You will be able to find appropriate projects for your students regardless of grade or ability levels.

★ - easy (Can be done by most students. Use as independent project for older students.)
★★ - medium (Can be done by younger students if done as step-by-step guided lessons.)
★★★ - difficult (Appropriate for third grade and up with some direction.)

▶ Introducing Techniques

It is important to teach the different techniques explained on pages 4 - 9. Once students understand how a technique works, you can refer to it by name rather than going through it step-by-step each time you introduce a project.

Model and have students practice the various folding and cutting techniques using a variety of paper types. In addition to building a background of skills to use, students can begin to get a feel for which techniques work best with the different papers - scrap paper, pieces of newspaper, tissue, tag, etc.

▶ Preparation for a Project

Read through the directions thoroughly before presenting any project to your students. Make a sample of the more complicated projects so you will be able to help students through any difficult spots.

It is also helpful to have all supplies needed for a project collected ahead of time. This allows you to concentrate on the art project.

▶ Guided Lessons

Guide students through the projects provided in this book. For some students, this guidance can be reading through the steps together and discussing any questions they might have. For others, you will need to model each step and have them follow along. In either case, when the guided project is completed, extend the activity by asking students to:

- try the same project with different types of paper
- do the lesson variations
- create their own art piece using the techniques practiced in the guided lesson

Paper Craft Center

▶ Center Set-Up

Place a table or bookshelf in front of the bulletin board. Use boxes and cans to hold scissors, paper, and other construction materials. Pin center standards and directions for projects to the bulletin board.

Paper:

construction	brown paper	tissue
wrapping paper	wall paper	foil
newspaper	cardstock	tagboard
thin cardboard	waxed paper	origami

Other Materials:

glue	glue	scissors
hole punch	glitter	stickers
yarn	string	raffia
pipe cleaners	paper plates	found objects

▶ Project Directions

Encourage students to explore the different materials and to create their own paper craft projects. Pin "challenge cards" to the bulletin board to help students get started on a project. Write each challenge on a 9" x 12" sheet of construction paper. Keep the challenge appropriate for the level of your students. Here are some challenges you might use.

- Make a greeting card for someone you like.
- Make a picture of plants and animals in the sea.
- Create a 3-D paper bridge going over a river.
- Make a mask of a character in your favorite story.
- Make a model of your house using only paper.
- Design a weaving using at least three types of paper.
- Make a scrapbook with a torn paper cover.
- Make a wild animal that is at least 3 feet (1 meter) tall.
- Design a new type of hand puppet.
- Make a place mat representing things about you.

Paper Craft Techniques
Pleat It - Curl It - Roll It

Pages 4-9 demonstrate techniques that will be used for projects in this book. Plan lessons specifically to practice these techniques. This will help the actual paper craft projects proceed more smoothly. Some techniques should be practiced in small groups. As techniques are learned, post and label samples on a bulletin board or chart so that students may refer to them later.

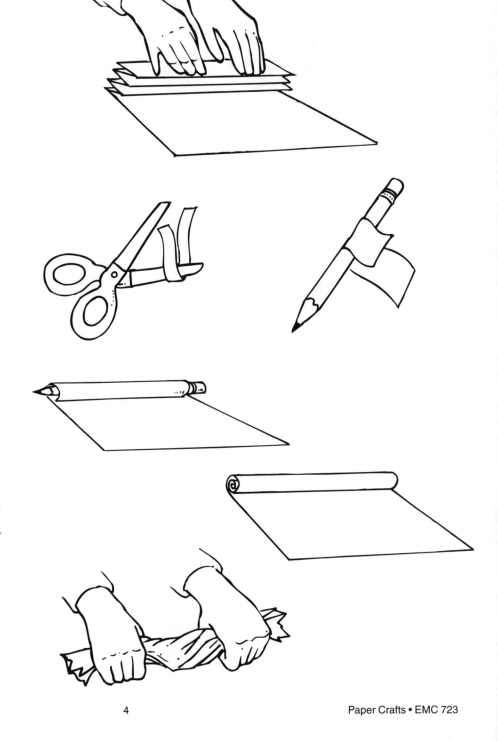

▶ Pleat/Fan
Any type of paper may be pleated, but thin paper is easier to fold. Experiment to see the difference in wide and narrow pleats.

▶ Curl
Paper can be curled using the edge of a pair of scissors or rolled over a pencil for a similar effect. (Very thick or very thin papers are difficult to curl.

▶ Roll or Twist
Rolling paper creates a smooth roll. Twisting paper creates a roll with texture. Both rolls can be bent or tied together to create other objects. Roll or twist from one side of the paper to the other. Form hollow tubes by rolling paper around a pencil.

 Paper Crafts • EMC 723

Folding Techniques

Even simple folds need to be practiced with younger students. Do paper folding at math time for practice with fractional parts.

▶ Halves - side to side

Lift one side of the paper. Line it up with the opposite side. Smooth the paper to make it flat.

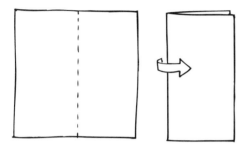

▶ Halves - corner to corner

Begin with a square. Lift one corner of the square. Lay it on top of the point of the opposite corner. Line up the sides of the paper. Smooth the paper to make it flat.

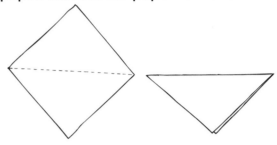

▶ Fourths - Eighths - Sixteenths

Fold the paper in half. Then fold it in half again. (Make one more fold for eighths and two more folds for sixteenths.)

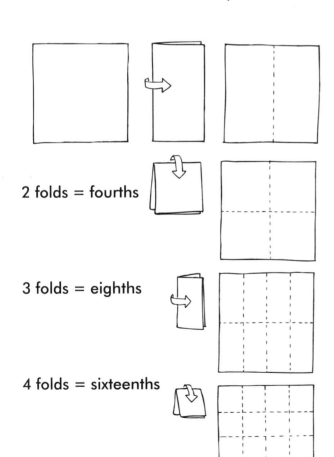

2 folds = fourths

3 folds = eighths

4 folds = sixteenths

▶ Thirds

Folding paper in thirds is difficult. You must either measure with a ruler or learn to approximate and adjust until you have thirds.

1. Have students loosely fold over the left side of the paper until the same amount of paper is covered by the fold as is still uncovered.
2. Without pressing down the fold, take the right side of the paper and fold it over.
3. If the folds are not the same size, carefully move the pieces back and forth to get them as close as possible.
4. When the folds look correct, smooth the paper to make it flat.

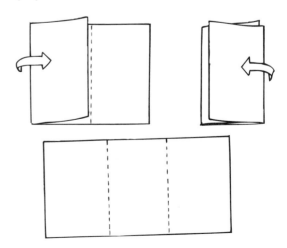

Paper Crafts • EMC 723

More Folding Techniques

▶ Score

Scoring makes it easier to bend paper for a 3-D effect. The point of a scissor or an opened paper clip can be used to score the paper. Press firmly, but not too hard. Gently bend paper along the score line.

▶ Accordion Fold

The accordion fold is made by folding strips of paper back and forth. The strip may be wide or narrow. Folds may be wide or narrow depending on how tight you want your "steps."

▶ Jacob's Ladder

Use two strips of paper that are the same width and length. Because you are folding paper over itself, you will need long strips. Strips can be the same or different colors.

1. Lay the two strips as shown and glue together.

2. Fold the top strip across to the left.

3. Fold the bottom strip up.

4. Fold the left strip to the right.

5. Fold the top strip down.

6. Continue until you reach the end of the strips. Cut off any excess and glue the ends together.

Scissor Techniques

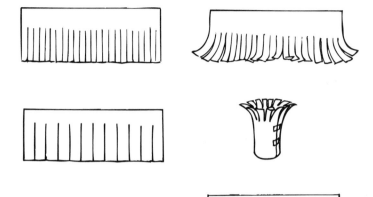

▶ Fringe

Fringe can be cut wide, narrow, long, or short to create different effects. The fringe can be curled or rolled up.

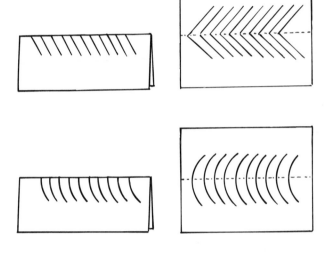

▶ Slits

Fold the paper and make short slanted or curved cuts. Open the paper and fold up the slits to add design or texture to your project.

▶ Rectangle to Square

Take hold of one corner of a rectangle. Pull the corner over until the short side of the paper is lined up with the long side. Cut along the line this makes.

▶ Rounding Corners

Circles and ovals don't always have to be perfectly shaped to work in an art project. Rounding the corners of a square or a rectangle is a quick way to create a circle or rectangle.

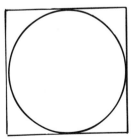
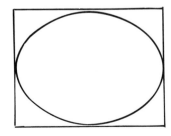

Young students need lots of practice with this technique. Tell them to start in the middle of a side and cut up "the hill" to the middle of the next side.

Cutting Techniques

▶ Spiral

Begin with a circle of any size. Start at the outside edge and cut a curving line around and around until you reach the center. Spirals can be used for designs, for curls or on people or animals.

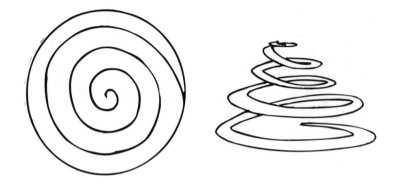

▶ Symmetrical Pieces

To create symmetrical shapes, begin with a folded piece of paper and cut both layers at the same time.

▶ Cutting in Series

Accordion fold a long strip of paper in an even number of folds. (You may want to measure first so you have exactly the same size sections each time.) The most important thing to remember is to leave an uncut section along each side.

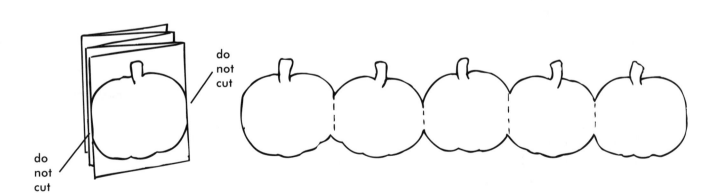

do not cut

do not cut

Special Techniques

▶ Tearing Paper

Tearing paper to make a desired shape or object is most easily done using a pinching and tearing motion. With one hand pinch the paper at the point you wish to make the tear. With the other hand slowly rip the paper. Move the pinching fingers along the line you wish the tear to follow. Some students will be able to tear out a picture freehand. Others will need to line sketch to follow.

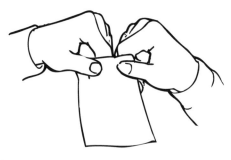

▶ Make a Cone

Begin with a circle of paper. Cut a slit from the edge of the circle to the center. Overlap the circle. (The farther you overlap the pieces the narrower the cone.) Tape the cone together.

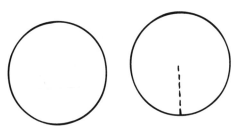

▶ 3-D Attachment Using Tabs

1. Fold over a part of the art work to make a tab. Glue down the tab only.

2. Cut slits along the edge to be attached to another piece. Fold the slits out to form tabs. Put tacky glue on the underside of the tabs. Hold the piece in place briefly to make the attachment.

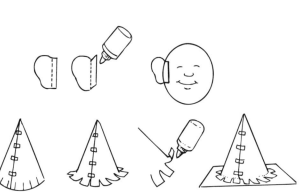

▶ Adding Texture to Paper

Before using a sheet of paper, add texture in one of the following ways:

1. Crumple the paper. Smooth it out with your fingers.

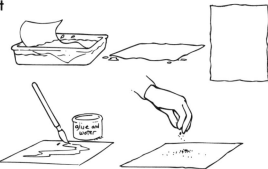

2. Wet the paper. Squeeze gently to remove water. Lay out the paper, but do not smooth it. Let the paper dry. This gives a rougher texture than the previous technique.

3. Place the paper over a rough surface such as a tree trunk, sidewalk, rough sandpaper, etc. and rub firmly with the side of a crayon.

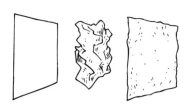

4. Cover the paper with a thin coat of glue mixed with water. Sprinkle on sand, glitter, cornmeal, etc. and let dry.

Paper Mosaic

Create simple designs or complicated scenes using small pieces of construction paper.

▶ Materials:
- 1" (2.5 cm) squares of paper in assorted colors
- glue
- scissors
- white construction paper - 9" x 12" (23 x 30.5 cm)
- pencil

Optional - Small squares cut from: printed wallpaper, gift wrap, foil papers

Note: Use muffin tins to organize squares by color. Children working at the same table can share a tin.

1. Lightly sketch the parts of your design or picture on the white construction paper. Keep the sketch simple.

2. Fill in each area using colored paper squares. Cut the squares into smaller pieces as needed. (Advanced students will be able to do some shading if several shades of one color are available.)

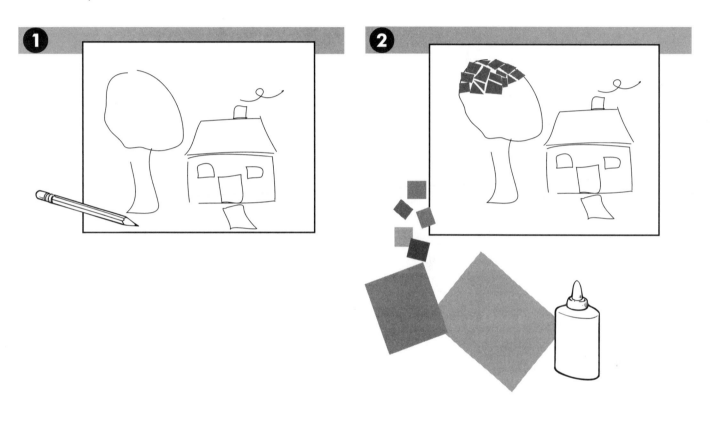

Tip - It is easier and neater to put glue on the white paper rather than the paper squares. Put glue only one section of your paper at a time.

Variation:

Tear paper into small pieces to make a mosaic picture. Provide paper of several types (construction, origami, wrapping paper, etc.) and sizes (6" [15 cm] and smaller). Follow steps one and two, tearing instead of cutting to create a picture.

Paper Weaving

Paper weaving is appropriate for all levels of ability. Simple weaving projects challenge children with immature motor skills. Older children are challenged by the many ways a flat piece of paper and paper strips can be combined.

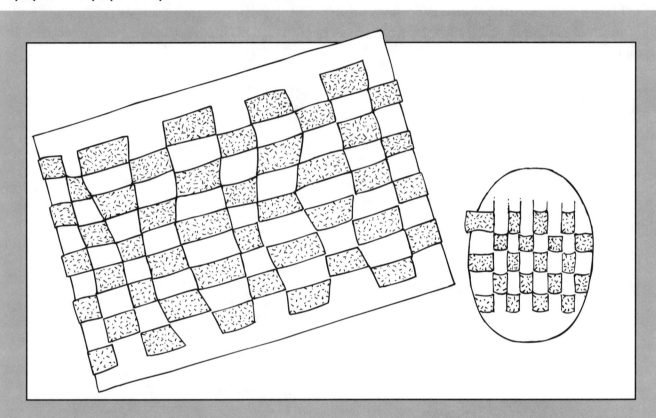

These weavings can be used as colorful place mats, to decorate greeting cards, and as additions to other works of art. Provide several types of paper to encourage creativity and variety.

▶ Materials:
- construction paper - different sizes and colors
- paper strips - different widths and lengths
- scissors
- glue
- ruler
- pencil

Note: The strips of paper need to be as long as the width of the largest size of construction paper you are using. Children can shorten the paper strips if necessary.

Steps to Follow:

1. Fold a sheet of flat paper in half. Make a line at least 1/2" (1.5 cm) from the open edge.

2. Cut from the folded edge to the line in a variety of ways.

3. Select one or more colors of strips. Weave the strips in and out.

4. Finish weaving. Trim any excess paper and glue the ends down.

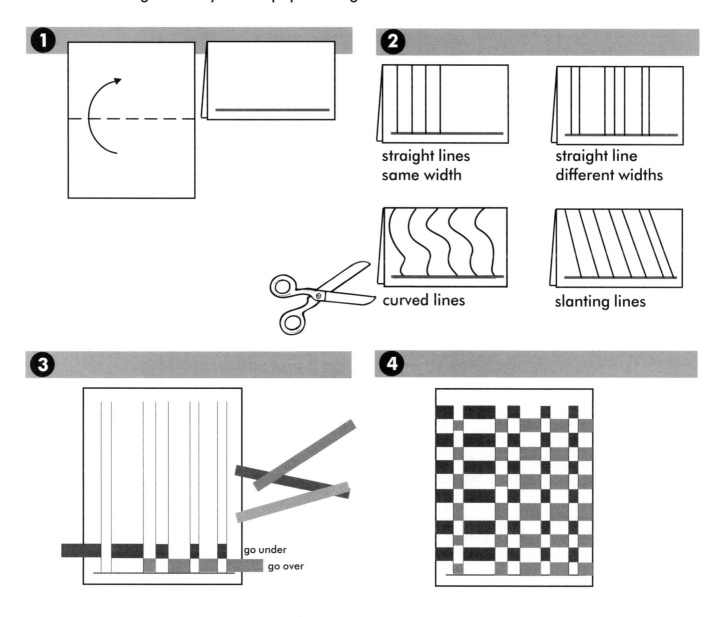

1

2

straight lines
same width

straight line
different widths

curved lines

slanting lines

3

go under
go over

4

Paper Lace

Paper lace can be used for placemats, added to greeting cards, used as backgrounds for other types of artwork, or used to decorate the room for a celebration.

▶ **Materials:**
- scissors
- paper - any size rectangle
  (Thinner papers such as copy paper or origami paper work better than heavy duty construction paper.)

Note: Have students practice with newspaper or inexpensive scratch paper until they know how to fold and cut without ending up with confetti.

Have first graders fold their paper as described in step one, and then cut designs freehand.

Steps to Follow:

1. Fold paper in quarters.

2. Cut freehand or sketch a simple design to cut.

3. Cut out the design along any or all sides.

4. Carefully open the paper lace to see the completed design.

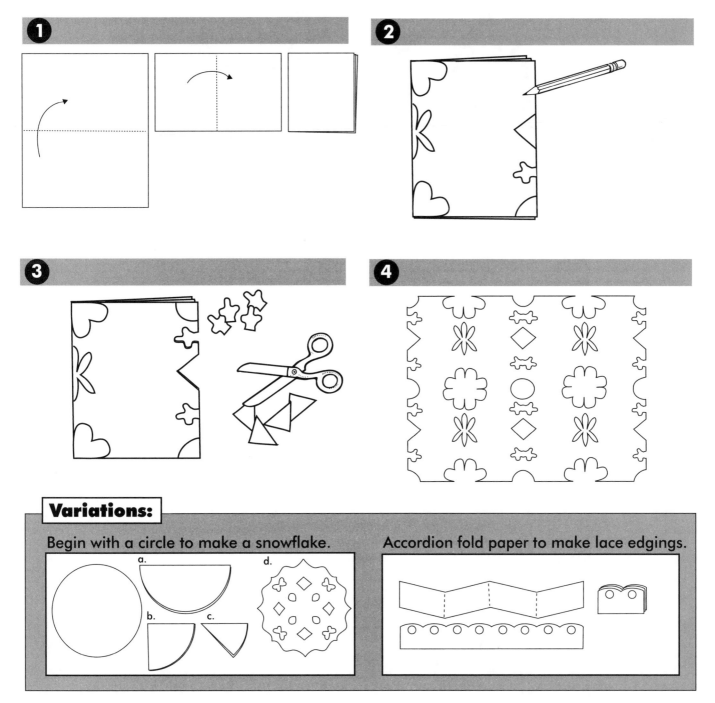

Variations:

Begin with a circle to make a snowflake.

Accordion fold paper to make lace edgings.

Silhouettes

Silhouettes are another interesting way to create art using scissors and paper. Simple objects or complex scenes can be cut from black paper. Black silhouettes glued to a colorful background are especially attractive.

▶ **Materials:**
- black construction paper - squares and rectangles in various sizes
- any color construction paper - 9" x 12" (23 x 30.5 cm)
- scissors
- glue or glue
- white crayon

▶ **Techniques to Use:**
Symmetrical pieces, page 8

1. Have students experiment with picture layout by placing various sizes of black paper on their background papers.

2. Sketch the object to be cut on the black paper with a white crayon. (If something symmetrical   is to be cut, fold the paper in half first.)

3. Cut out the silhouettes.

4. Glue cut-outs to the background paper to create a scene in silhouette.

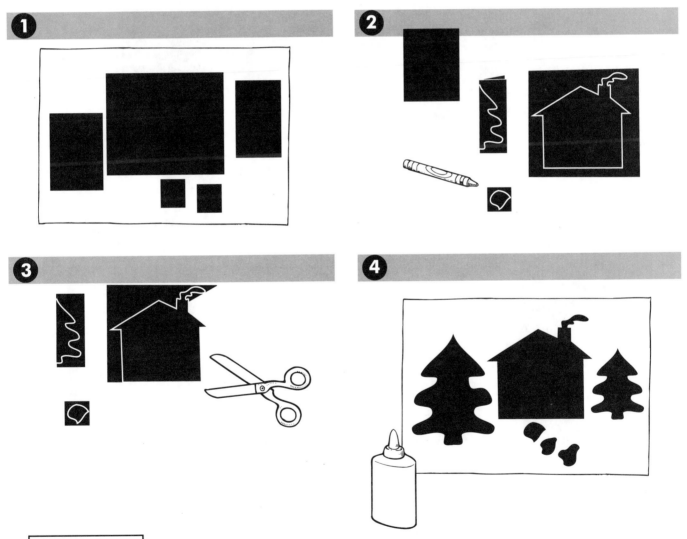

Positive-Negative Pictures

This quick and easy technique results in a lovely night scene of snow-covered trees and their shadows in the snow. Children may create one or more types of trees for their forests.

▶ Materials:
- construction paper
  - white - 12" x 18" (30.5 x 45.7 cm)
  - black - 6" x 18" (15 x 45.5 cm)
- white or yellow crayon
- scissors
- glue

Optional - Add stick-on stars to the night sky.

Steps to Follow:

1. Sketch a line of tree shapes with a crayon. The base of the tree must come to the lower edge of the black paper. Trees don't need to be the same height.

2. Cut out the trees following your crayon line.

3. Glue the black night-sky paper to the top half of the white paper WITHOUT the cut-out trees.

4. Now lay the trees back in their original spots. Put glue on the fronts (one tree at a time) and carefully flip the tree down to form a shadow of the snow-covered tree. Be sure the base lines of the tree and its shadow line up. Glue the rest of the tree shadows down.

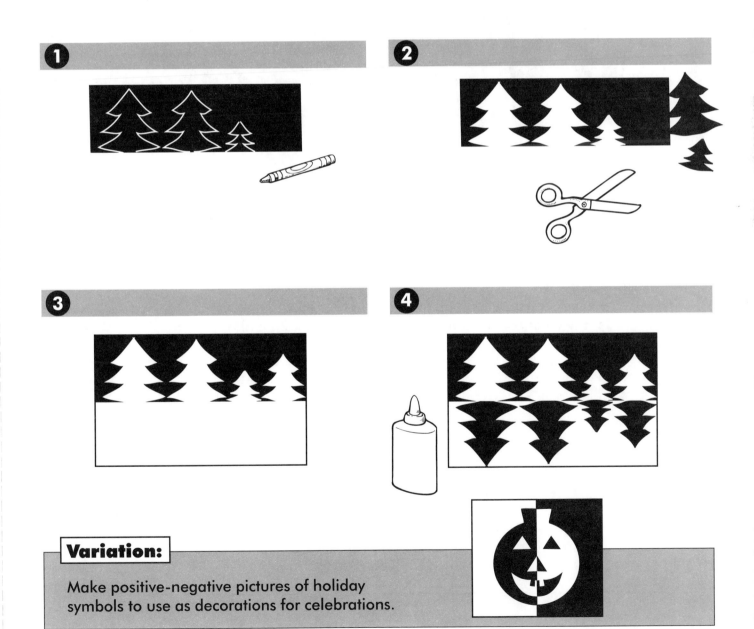

Variation:

Make positive-negative pictures of holiday symbols to use as decorations for celebrations.

Cut-Out Picture

Cut-out pictures take silhouettes one step farther, adding details cut from within the boundaries of the shape. Small scissors with pointed tips are essential if children are doing anything complicated.

▶ **Materials:**
- black construction paper - 4" x 6" (10 x 15 cm)
- any color construction paper - 6" x 9" (15 x 23 cm)
- white crayon
- scissors
- glue

Steps to Follow:

1. With a white crayon, sketch a piece of fruit with its stem and leaves on the black paper.

2. Cut out the fruit.

3. Decide which inside parts will be cut out and sketch these in with the white crayon.

4. Poke the scissors into the inside area to be cut out. Take your time and cut carefully.

5. Use scraps to cut out seeds for the fruit.

6. Glue the main silhouette on your background paper. Glue the seeds to the inside of the fruit.

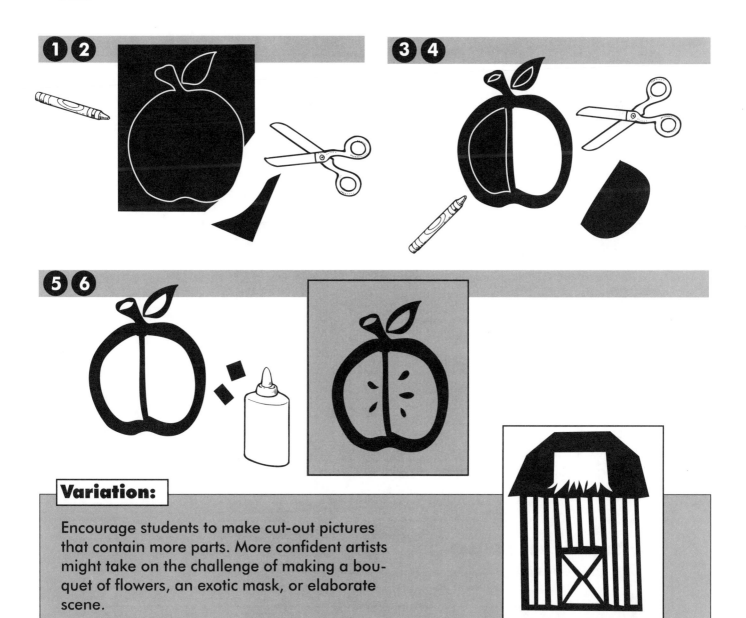

Variation:

Encourage students to make cut-out pictures that contain more parts. More confident artists might take on the challenge of making a bouquet of flowers, an exotic mask, or elaborate scene.

Paper Chain People

No matter what your age, it's always exciting to open up your paper and find that you succeeded in creating a chain of shapes. Cutting in series requires children to follow a few rules, but once these have been mastered, the sky's the limit.

▶ Materials:
- any color paper - 4" x 12" (10 x 30.5 cm) paper
- scissors
- pencil
- crayons

Note: Thin, but not delicate, paper such as lightweight shelf paper, copy paper, wrapping paper, etc. works best if your chain is going to be very long. Construction paper gets too thick to cut after only a few folds.

▶ Techniques to Use:
Cutting in series, page 8

Steps to Follow:

1. Put a mark every 1 1/2" (3.8 cm) along the paper to serve as a folding guide.

2. Accordion fold the paper.

3. Sketch 1/2 of a person with the middle of the body along one fold and a foot and hand touching the other fold.

4. Cut out the person and carefully open up the chain.

5. Add facial details and clothing using crayons.

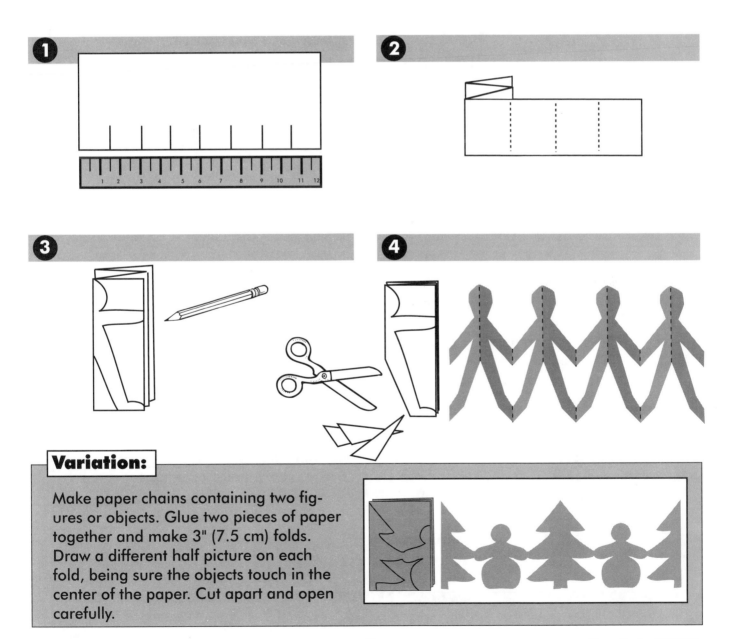

Variation:

Make paper chains containing two figures or objects. Glue two pieces of paper together and make 3" (7.5 cm) folds. Draw a different half picture on each fold, being sure the objects touch in the center of the paper. Cut apart and open carefully.

★★ Cut Paper People

Cut paper pictures with their bright colors and interesting prints make a nice change from crayons and paint. Encourage children to use both solid and print papers. Add a few special kinds such as bright origami paper, foils, etc. to your supply.

▶ Materials:

- construction paper for background - 9" x 12" (23 x 30.5 cm)
- scratch paper for planning
- an assortment of papers in different sizes, types, and colors
- pencil
- scissors
- glue

Note: Share books that have been illustrated with cut paper to inspire your artists. Books by Eric Carle and Leo Lionni are good examples of using cut and torn paper to create pictures.

1. Decide on the person to be made (someone from history, a story you've read, your own life, etc.).

2. Make a rough sketch of the person using pencil on scratch paper. This rough sketch will act as a guide as you complete the picture. It should be big enough to fill your whole paper. It should contain only the most important parts of the final picture. (See sketches below.)

3. Collect scraps of paper in the colors needed for the picture. You can determine the size needed for each element by laying the paper over the part of the rough sketch it will be used for.

4. Cut the parts freehand or sketch the shape lightly with a pencil and then cut out.

5. Arrange all pieces on the background paper. When everything is in place, glue the pieces to the paper.

6. Add details using smaller pieces of paper. Use marking pens for details too small to cut.

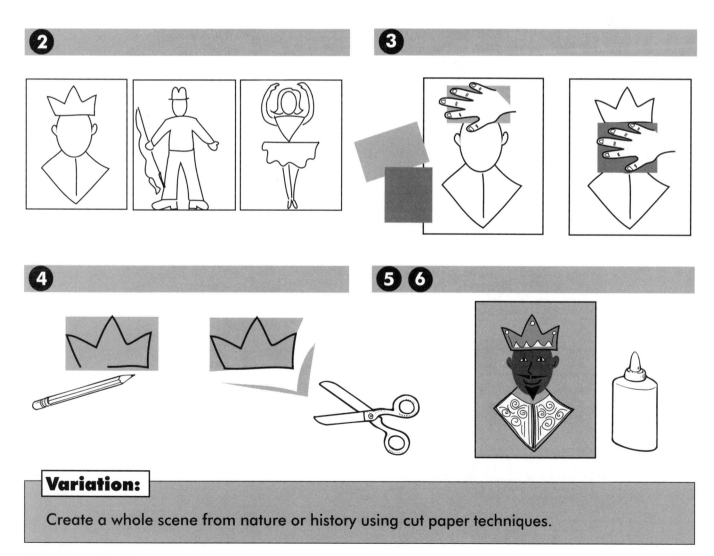

Variation:

Create a whole scene from nature or history using cut paper techniques.

Torn Paper Still Life

Torn paper adds a special texture to pictures. Creating a still life of fruit is a good place to begin, since the elements are all large and uncomplicated. After some practice children will be ready to tackle more complicated projects. Shading can be added with crayons or colored chalk to give the still life a more finished look.

▶ Materials:
- black construction paper - 12" x 18" (30.5 x 45.5 cm)
- paper - an assortment of bright colors
  - 6" x 9" (15 x 23 cm)
  - 4" x 6" (10 x 15 cm)
- scraps
- scissors
- glue
- pencil
- crayons or colored chalk

Note: Origami paper, wrapping paper, etc. make the most attractive pictures as their colors are usually more intense than construction paper.

▶ Techniques to Use:
Torn paper, page 9

Steps to Follow:

1. Decide on the shape of the container that will hold the fruit. Tear out the container shape from a 6" x 9" (15 x 23 cm) piece of paper. (Sketch the shape lightly with a pencil if you need to. Tear along your sketch line.)

2. Decide what fruit will go in your container. Select the colors you need. Tear each piece out carefully. Tear stems and leaves for some of the fruit.

3. Arrange the container and fruit on the black construction paper. When you are happy with your arrangement, glue the pieces down.

4. Add details and shadows with crayons or colored chalk.

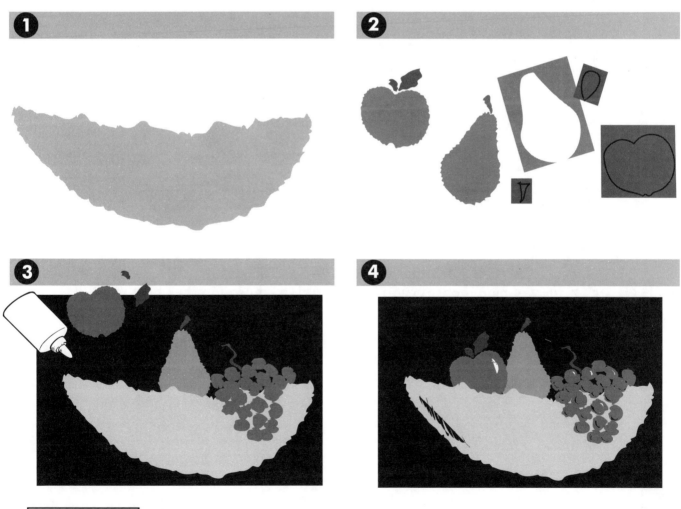

Variation:

Make a face, animal, or scene using pieces of torn paper.

27   Paper Crafts • EMC 723

Origami Whale

A few simple folds turns a square of paper into a charming whale. Change the size of the square to make larger or smaller whales. Have students create interesting backgrounds for their whales.

▶ **Materials:**
- blue construction paper - 9" x 12" (23 x 30.5 cm)
- gray or black construction paper - 6" (15 cm) square
- crayons or marking pens
- scissors
- glue

Steps to Follow:

1. Begin with the 6" (15 cm) square. Follow the steps below.

2. Finish off the face of the whale with crayons or marking pens.

3. Glue the whale to the blue construction paper. (Think about what the whale is doing - diving,   spouting, breaching...) Add details such as water, other animals, sky, etc. to the background.

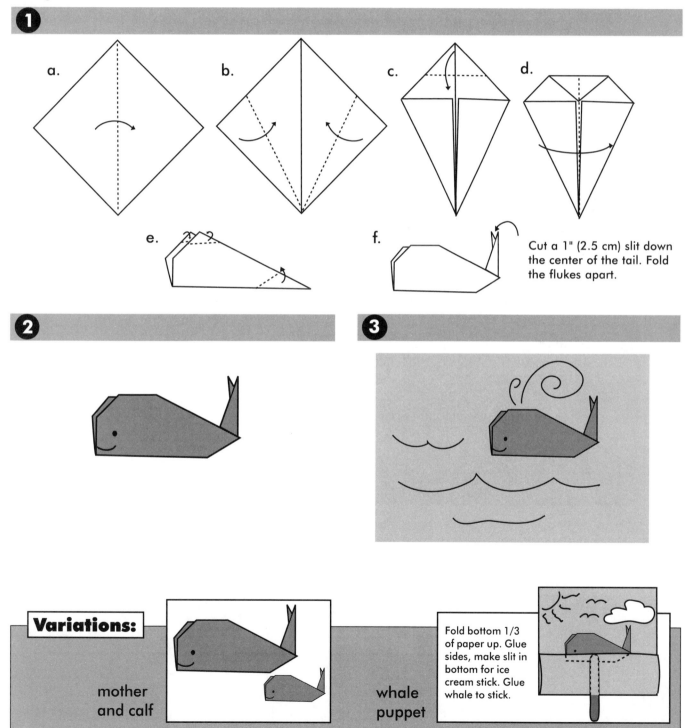

1

a.

b.

c.

d.

e.

f.

Cut a 1" (2.5 cm) slit down the center of the tail. Fold the flukes apart.

2

3

Variations:

mother and calf

whale puppet

Fold bottom 1/3 of paper up. Glue sides, make slit in bottom for ice cream stick. Glue whale to stick.

29   Paper Crafts • EMC 723

★★ Paper Mobiles

Almost anything can be placed on a mobile. Here are two simple versions students can use anytime they wish to watch their art work dance on the wind.

▶ Materials:

Paper Cone Mobile
- thin paper plate
- string - 12" (30.5 cm) - 5 pieces
  18" (45.5 cm) - 1 piece
- cellophane tape
- pencil
- hole punch
- optional - hole reinforcers

Straw Mobile
- 3 drinking straws
- string - 18" (45.5) - 5 pieces

Items On Mobile
- construction paper scraps - various colors and sizes
- scissors
- glue
- crayons or marking pens
- hole punch

Optional - Reproduce the patterns on page 32.

▶ Techniques to Use:

Cone, page 9

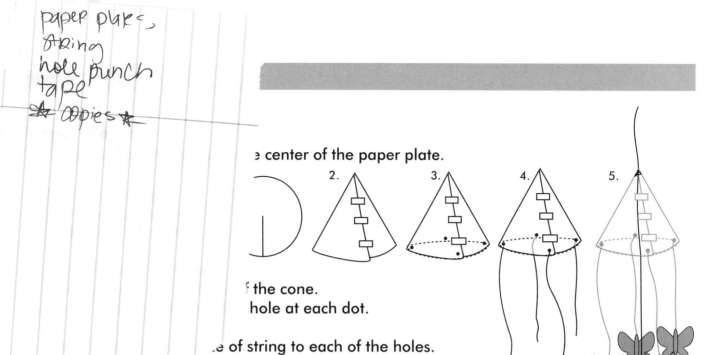

center of the paper plate.

the cone.

hole at each dot.

of string to each of the holes.

d.

piece of string up through the top of the cone.
Tie it to the remaining 12" (30.5 cm) piece as shown below.
It will hang down from the middle of the mobile.

Drinking Straws

1. Put a piece of string through each of the straws.

2. Tie the straws together.

3. Tie one string to the center of the top straw.

4. Tie the last string to the top straw.
   Use this string to hang the mobile.

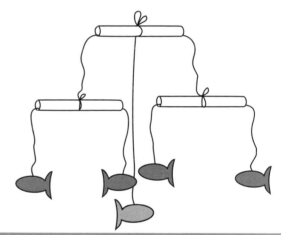

Objects on Mobile

Use the patterns on page 32 or make your own as follows:

1. Cut five pieces of construction paper into shapes for the mobile.
   Make all the shapes the same, or use several shapes.

2. Decide what topic to show on the mobile (animals, vehicles, family
   members, state facts, etc.). Draw pictures on both sides of each shapes.

3. Punch holes in each of the shapes. Tie a shape to each string
   on the mobile.

Variation:

Make small origami butterflies, birds, or fish to hang from the mobile.

Note: Reproduce these patterns to use with the mobile on page 31.

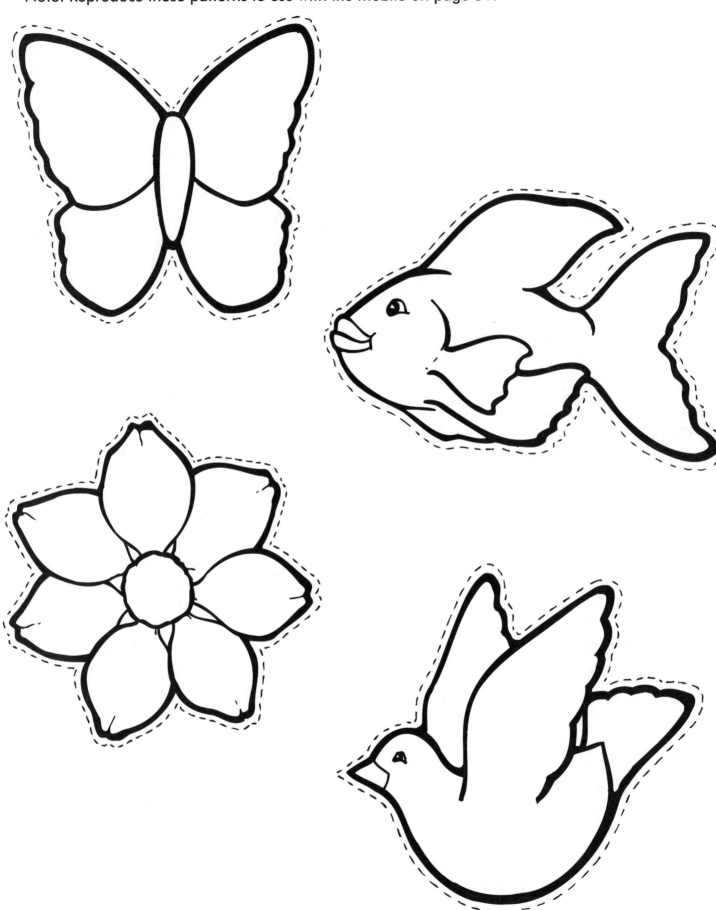

Paper Crafts • EMC 723

Note: Challenge students to make a picture using two or more of the techniques they have learned for folded paper. Brainstorm to create a list of possibilities. Provide a variety of types, sizes, and colors of paper.

Challenge
Paper Craft

Name of Project ______________________________

Artist ______________________________

List your materials here:

______________ ______________

______________ ______________

______________ ______________

______________ ______________

______________ ______________

______________ ______________

Write the steps you followed here:

1. ______________________________
____
2. ______________________________
____
3. ______________________________
____
4. ______________________________
____
5. ______________________________
____
6. ______________________________
____

Use the back of this page if you need more space.
Put this form with your finished project.

Paper Lanterns

Paper lanterns are a colorful addition to your room environment for special occasions. Designs can be added using cut paper scraps, crayons, or marking pens. Add tassels made from bits of string. Use different color combinations to make lanterns for a variety of holidays: orange and black for Halloween; red, white, and green for Christmas, red for Valentine's Day, etc.

▶ Materials:
- bright colored paper - 9" x 12" (23 x 30.5 cm)
- 2 pieces of string - 15" (38 cm)
- pencil
- scissors
- crayons or marking pens
- glue
- hole punch

▶ Techniques to Use:
Slits, page 7

Paper Crafts • EMC 723

Steps to Follow:

1. Fold paper in half the long way.

2. Make a line one inch in along the open side. This is a cutting guide.

3. Cut slits about 1" apart from the fold to the pencil line.

4. Draw a design along the uncut edge on both sides.

5. Unfold the paper. Bend the ends around and glue them together to form the lantern.

6. Punch two holes on opposite sides of the top of the lantern. Tie a string in each hole. Knot the strings together at the other end.

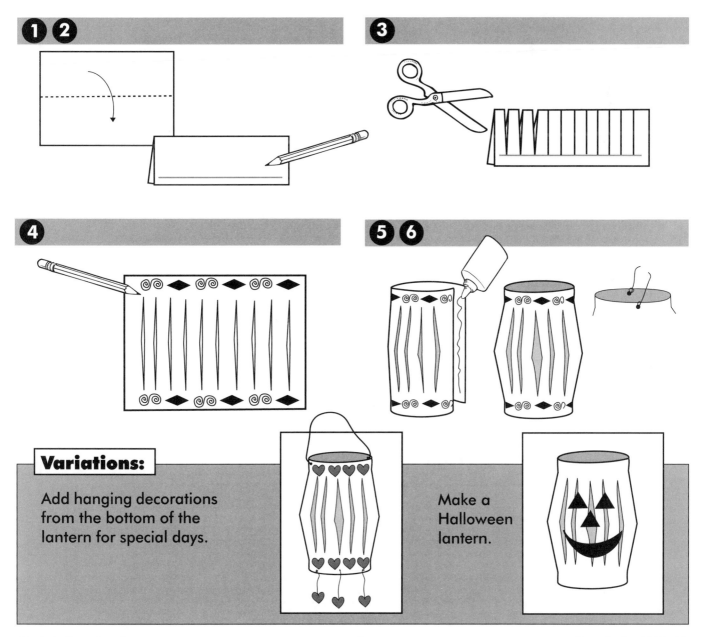

Variations:

Add hanging decorations from the bottom of the lantern for special days.

Make a Halloween lantern.

Snail Trail

A bit of folded paper plus a spiral of color and you have a delightful snail. Add a 3-D leaf and a shiny trail to complete this small work of art.

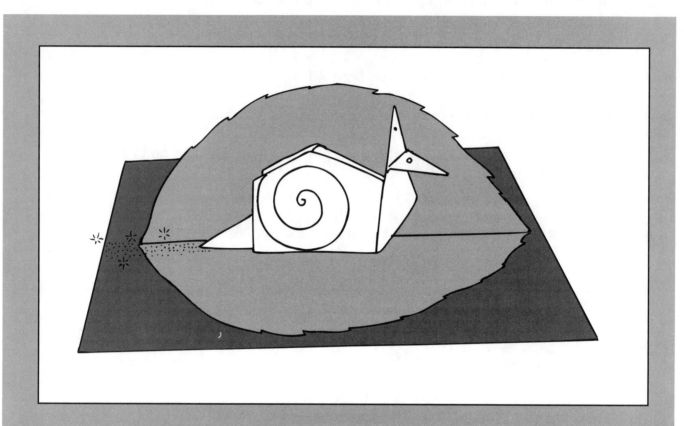

▶ Materials:

- brown construction paper - 9" x 12" (23 x 30.5 cm) - background
- green construction paper - 6" x 9" (15 x 23 cm) - leaf
- copier paper or origami paper - 6" (15 cm) - snail
- marking pens or crayons
- scissors
- glue

Optional - white or clear glitter for the snail's trail

▶ Techniques to Use:

Score, page 6

Snail

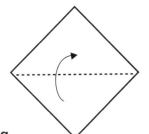

a.
fold in half, corner to corner, then re-open

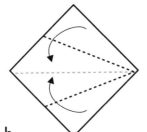

b.
fold in to center line

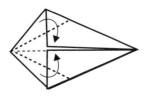

c.
fold top and bottom points in to center line

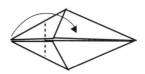

d.
fold left point in

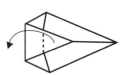

e.
fold back out

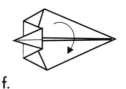

f.
fold in half, from top to bottom

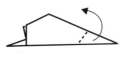

g.
fold right point up in 90 degree angle

h.
cut the tip along fold line about 1" (2.5 cm), fold one section out to make snail's tentacles

i.
add snail's shell and eyes with crayons or markers

Leaf

1. Cut out a free-form leaf. Make it as big as possible.

2. Score the leaf with scissors or an opened paper clip. Crease the leaf along the score line and bend to make it 3-D.

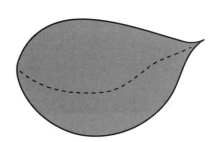

3. Glue the snail to half the leaf.

Background

Glue the other half of the leaf to the brown background.

Optional - Make a glue trail from the end of the snail, off the leaf, and across the "ground." Sprinkle it with glitter.

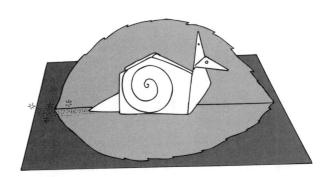

Variation:

Make only the snails. Then put a paper vine up one wall of the classroom. Attach all of the snails to the vine.

Paper Crafts • EMC 723

3-D Paper Lace Decoration

This project is bound to elicit loud "oos" and "wows" as students pull open their cut paper and see the cascade of paper lace. Hang these around the room to decorate for special events or parties.

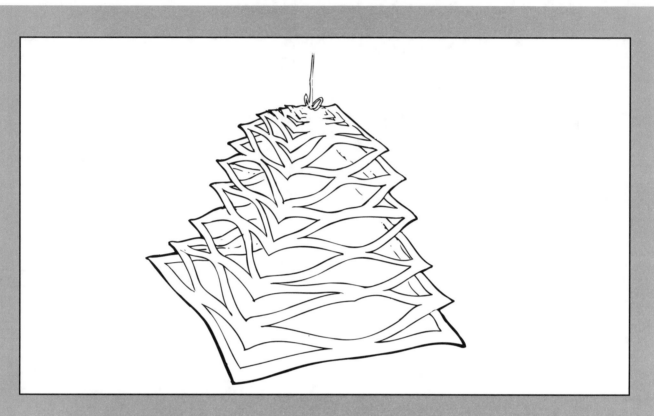

▶ Materials:
- copier or typing paper - 6" (15 cm) square
- string - 12" (30.5 cm) piece

Note: It is very important to carefully pull the pieces apart or you will have a torn piece of paper rather than a delightful, lacy decoration.

▶ Techniques to Use:
Fold corner to corner, page 5
Slits, page 7

Steps to Follow:

1. Follow folds a-c.

2. Cut slits about 1/2" (1.75 cm) apart along the folded side. Cut almost to the other side. (Take the time to do this carefully. The design will be ruined if you cut all the way through.)

3. Make a second set of cuts along the other side. Hold the paper firmly as you cut.

4. Carefully unfold the paper until it is flat.

5. Pinch the center and gently pull down each corner.

6. Poke a hole in the top center. Put the string through the hole. Make a large knot to hold it in place. Hang the decoration by the other end.

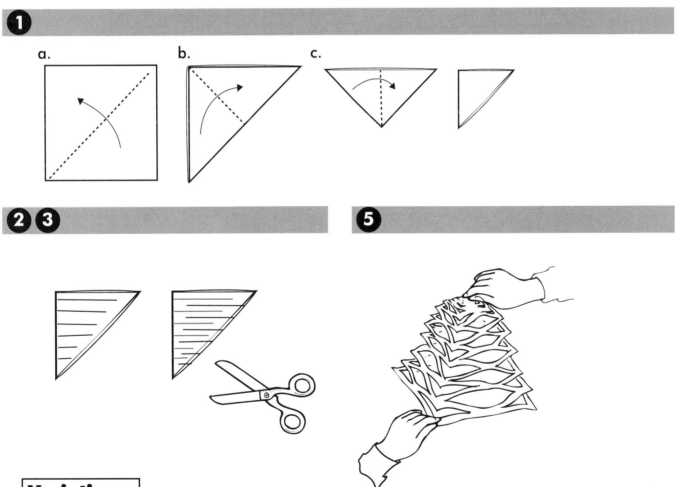

① a.   b.   c.

② ③   ⑤

Variations:

Make paper lace from squares of gold or silver foil wrapping paper. Use larger squares for hanging "lanterns" and smaller squares for ornaments to go on a Christmas tree. Use narrow ribbon or silver cord to hang the decorations.

Butterfly

Bring spring indoors with a beautiful bunch of butterflies made from pleated paper. A bit of pipe cleaner holds it all together and provides the butterfly's antennae.

 Materials:
- 6" (15 cm) paper square
- 4" (10 cm) paper square
- pipe cleaner - 7" (18 cm) piece
- cellophane tape

Note: Any paper will do. Origami paper, wrapping paper, construction paper, etc., will each give a different effect.

 Techniques to Use:
Pleats, page 4

Steps to Follow:

1. Fold the large square following steps a-e. Repeat the same steps with the small square.

2. Unfold the paper and pleat the paper up and down along the creases. Pinch the paper together in the center.

3. Tape the two pieces together.

4. Fold the pipe cleaner in half. Twist it around the center of the two pleated papers. Twist the ends of the pipe cleaner to form antennae.

5. Spread out the pleated paper to form the wings.

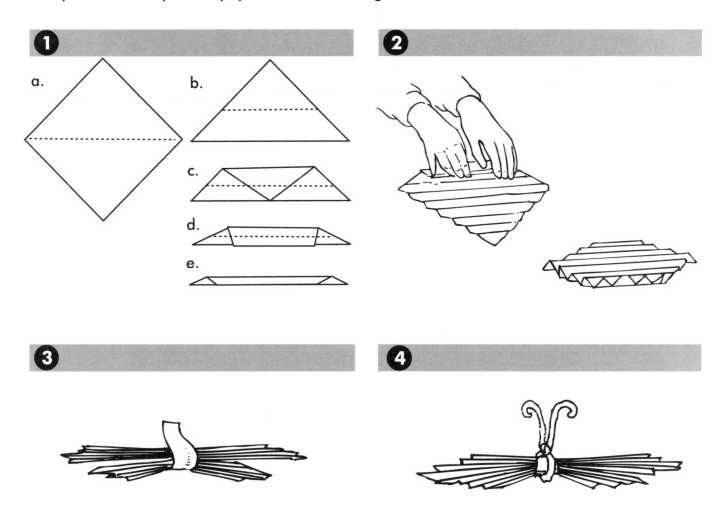

Variation:

Use only the 6" (15 cm) square to create a bow or bowtie. Use tape or ribbon to pinch the bow together in the center.

★ Paper Strip Abstract

Encourage students to use all of their paper bending, curling, pleating, etc. skills to create 3-D abstracts from strips of paper. Cardboard makes a sturdy base for this free-form work of art.

▶ Materials:

- one 9" x 12" (23 x 30.5 cm) piece of cardboard - for base
- construction paper - assorted colors
    - two 4 1/2" x 6" (12 x 15 cm) - for strips
    - four 3" (7.5 cm) squares - for circles
- scissors
- glue

▶ Techniques to Use:

Curl, Twist, page 4
Score, page 6
Fringe, Round, page 7
Spiral, page 8

Steps to Follow:

1. Cut the 4 1/2" x 6" (12 x 15 cm) paper into strips.

2. Round the corners of the squares to make circles.

3. Glue the strips and shapes to the cardboard base to create a 3-D design. Be creative and have fun!

1

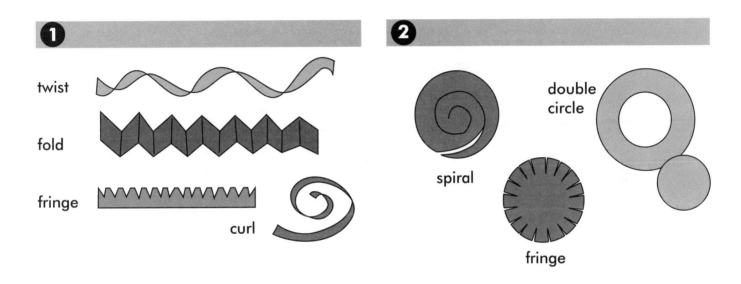

twist

fold

fringe

curl

2

spiral

double circle

fringe

3

Variation:

Provide extra paper for children who want to add other creative paper additions to their designs.

Paper Crafts • EMC 723

Paper Buildings

A flat sheet of paper folded into boxes can be converted into a quick three-dimensional building. Use different sizes of squares and rectangles to create different types of buildings.

▶ Materials:
- construction paper - 9" x 12" (23 x 30.5 cm)
- paper scraps in assorted colors
- scissors
- crayons
- pencil
- tape

▶ Techniques to Use:
Fold in sixteenths, page 5

1. Fold the paper 4 times to make 16 boxes.

2. Cut along the lines as shown. Use paper scraps and crayons to add windows and other details to both sides of the paper, creating the inside and outside scenes.

3. Fold and tape the roof. Tape both ends.

4. Fold and tape the sides of the house. Tape both ends.

5. Cut a door. Fold it open.

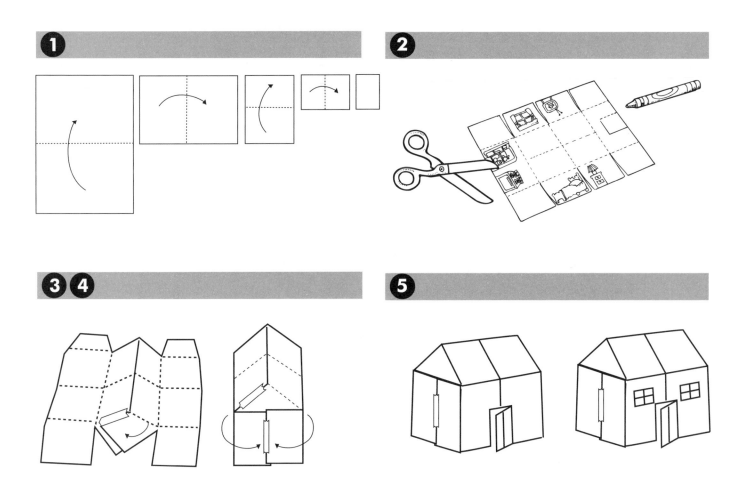

Variations:

The basic paper building directions can be used to create a log cabin, a cottage, a gingerbread house, etc.

Before taping the house together, cut out windows so you can peek inside the house.

★ Paper Hats

Hats for drama, hats for holidays, hats for fun. Try these folded paper hats as starters; then challenge your students to create their own.

▶ **Materials:**
- paper - 20" (51 cm) square
- scraps of colored paper
- scissors
- glue

Note: Use colored butcher paper, newspaper, or colorful wrapping paper for these hats.

Steps to Follow:

Hat 1

1. Fold the 20" (51 cm) square following steps a-g.

2. Cut dots, feathers, insignias, etc. out of construction paper. Glue these to your hat.

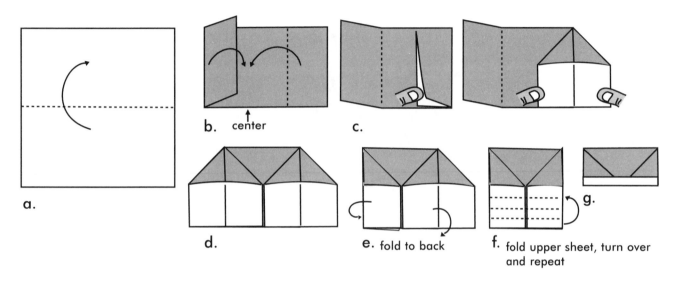

a.

b. center

c.

d.

e. fold to back

f. fold upper sheet, turn over and repeat

g.

Hat 2

1. Fold the 20" (51 cm) square following steps a-e.

2. Cut dots, feathers, insignias, etc. out of construction paper. Glue these to your hat.

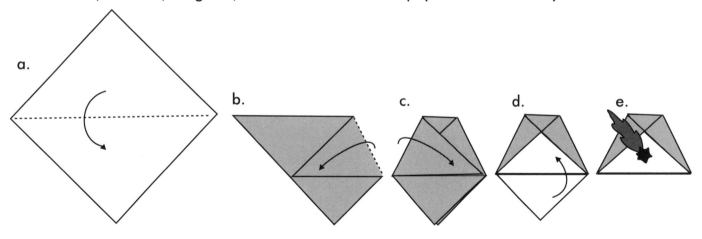

a.

b.

c.

d.

e.

Variation:

Have students create original hats from a 20" (51 cm) square. Encourage them to use found objects (buttons, leaves, feathers, ribbon, etc.) to decorate their hats.

Samurai Helmet

The Samurai helmet is a great addition to your "hat-making" repertoire. Use plain paper for a helmet or bright printed paper for a party hat.

► **Materials:**
  • paper 20" (51 cm) square

Optional for party hats –   • scraps of colored paper
  • scissors
  • glue

Fold the 20" (51 cm) paper square following steps a-j:

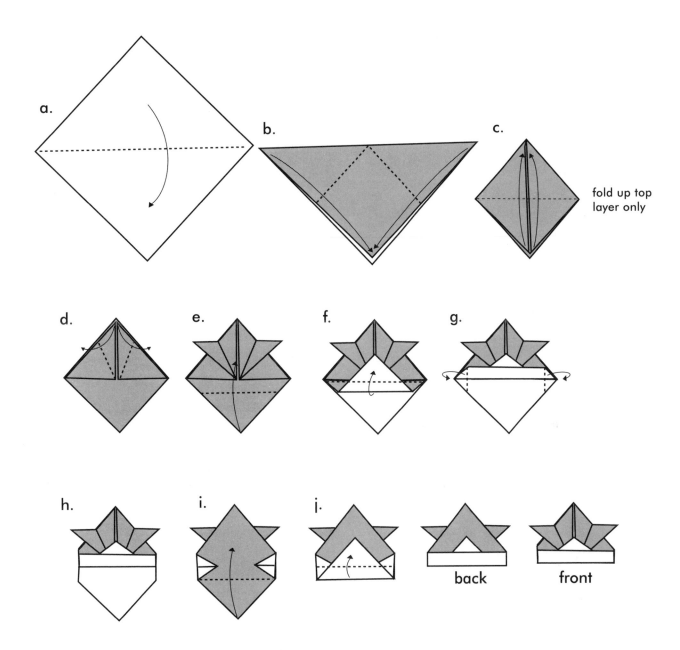

a.

b.

c. fold up top
layer only

d.

e.

f.

g.

h.

i.

j.

back

front

Folded Paper Puppets

★★ Frog   Bird ★★★

A simple paper fold can be transformed into a myriad of hand puppets. For practice, have your students make a funny frog and an exotic tropical bird.

▶ Materials:

Frog Materials:
- green construction paper
    - 9" x 18" (23 x 45.5 cm) - body
    - 9" x 12" (23 x 30.5 cm) - body parts
- black construction paper - 1" x 2" (2.5 x 5 cm) - pupils
- thin red construction paper scrap - tongue
- copy of body parts patterns (page 53)
- 2 cotton balls
- markers or crayons
- scissors, glue

Bird Materials:
- construction paper
    - purple - 9" x 18" (23 x 45.5 cm) - puppet base
    - red - 6" (15 cm) square - bird body
    - blue - 6" (15 cm) square - bird tail
    - 2 orange - 3" x 7" (7.5 x 18 cm) - wings
    - black - 2" x 8" (5 x 20 cm) - eyes, beak
- copy of body parts patterns (page 55)
- 2 cotton balls
- markers or crayons
- scissors, glue

Begin with a 9" x 18" (23 x 45.5 cm) piece of construction paper.

Steps to follow:

a. Fold in thirds lengthwise.

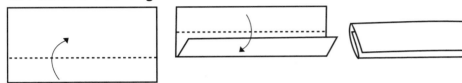

b. Flip paper over.

c. Fold in half.

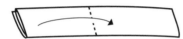

d. Fold top edge back to meet the fold.

e-f. Flip over. Fold top edge back to meet the fold. Fold.

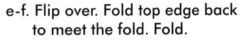

g. Fingers go in the open ends.

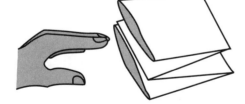

▶ Techniques to Use:
Fold in thirds, page 5

Steps to Follow for Frog:

1. Make the basic puppet out of the green construction paper.

2. Cut out the pattern pieces and trace them on construction paper. (See page 53.) Cut out the pieces.

3. Assemble as shown.

1

2

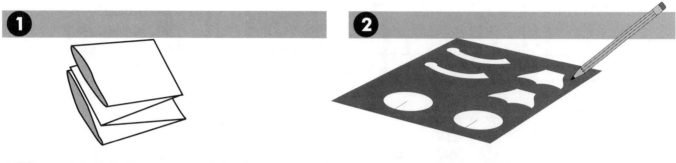

3

a. Accordion fold legs and glue a foot at the end of each leg. Glue legs onto the bottom fold of puppet body.

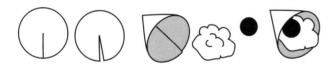

b. Glue each arm underneath the first fold of puppet body.

c. Slit circle (eyelid), form into a cone shape. Glue cottonball and pupil into place. Glue eyes on top of puppet body.

d. Curl a piece of thin red scrap paper, and glue in mouth.

▶ **Techniques to Use:**
Curl, page 4
Accordion Fold, page 6
Cone, page 9

Variation:

Make frog's friend toad. Use brown paper to make the puppet. Add spots with dark brown marking pen or crayon.

 Paper Crafts • EMC 723

Frog Parts

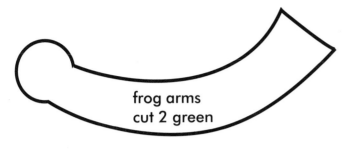

frog arms
cut 2 green

frog foot
cut 2 green

frog eyelid
cut 2 green

slit

frog pupils black

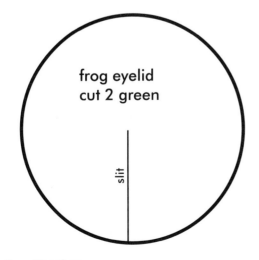

frog arms
cut 2 green

frog foot
cut 2 green

frog eyelid
cut 2 green

slit

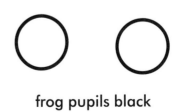

frog pupils black

Paper Crafts • EMC 723

Steps to Follow for Bird:

1. Make the basic puppet out of the purple construction paper.

2. Cut out the pattern pieces and trace them on appropriate colors of paper. Cut out the pieces. (See page 55.)

3. Assemble as shown.

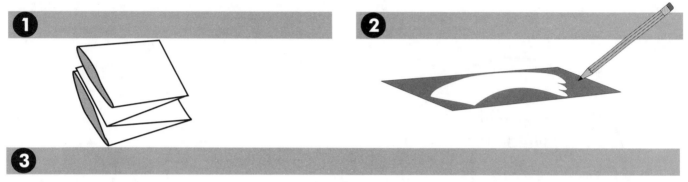

3

a. Glue the beak to the folded end of the basic puppet.

b. Glue the red square to the basic puppet. Then glue the blue square to the end of the red square.

c. Fold the two squares as shown to make the bird's body and tail. Fringe the blue section to make the bird's tail.

d-e. Glue the wings to the body. Use cotton balls for whites of eyes. Glue on the black pupils. Add details such as feathers with markers or crayons.

▶ **Techniques to Use:**
Fringe, page 7
3-D Attachment, page 9

Variation:

Challenge students to create their own puppets starting with the basic puppet as the base.

Tropical Bird Parts

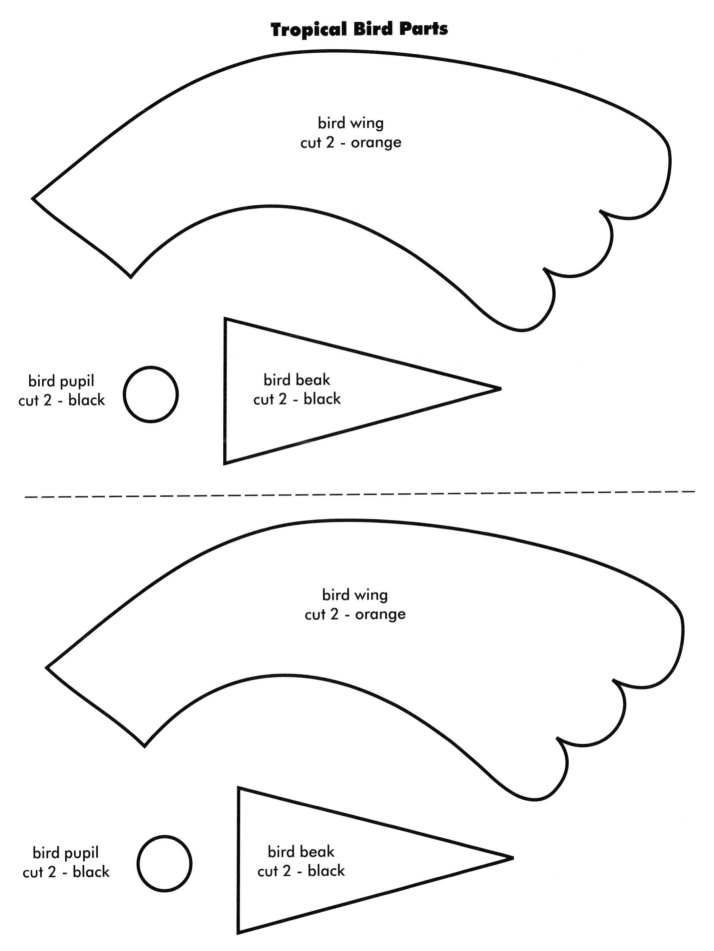

bird wing
cut 2 - orange

bird pupil
cut 2 - black

bird beak
cut 2 - black

bird wing
cut 2 - orange

bird pupil
cut 2 - black

bird beak
cut 2 - black

Paper "Mitt" Puppet

Here is another basic form that can be used to create all sorts of paper puppets. Have children create the funny space creature for practice, then turn them loose to design their own.

▶ Materials:

- green construction paper
  - 9" x 12" (23 x 30.5 cm) - basic puppet
  - 4 - 1" x 6" (2.5 x 15 cm) - arms
- yellow construction paper
  - 3" x 4" (7.5 x 10 cm) - mouth
  - 2 - 2" (5 cm) squares - eyes
  - 2 - 1/2" x 2 1/2" (1.5 x 6.5 cm) - eye holders
- purple construction paper
  - 2 - 1" x 3" (2.5 x 7.5 cm) - legs
  - 2 - 3" x 4" (7.5 x 10 cm) - feet
- 2" (5 cm) piece of pipe cleaner - antennae
- crayons
- scissors
- glue

▶ Techniques to Use:

Accordion Fold, page 6
Rounding Corners, page 7

Basic Mitt Directions :

Use the 9" x 12" (23 x 30.5 cm) piece of green construction paper.

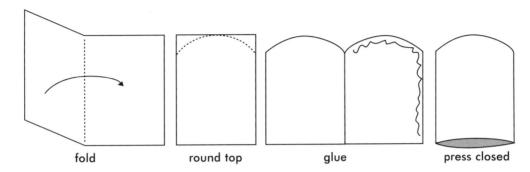

fold   round top   glue   press closed

Space Creature

Assemble as shown.

a. Eyes: round the corners then draw on pupils. Accordion fold rectangular strips, glue to eyeball then glue to top of head.

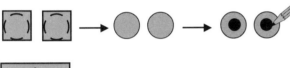

b. Mouth: sketch a mouth shape. Cut out. Add details with crayons. Glue to face.

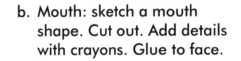

c. Arms: Fringe one end of each strip, accordion fold, glue to back.

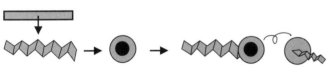

d. Legs and feet: cut out feet, glue to legs, then glue legs to inside front of puppet.

e-f. Add the polka dots using a marking pen or dots cut from paper scraps. Add the antennae: glue or tape on back

                   Paper Crafts • EMC 723

Paper Plate Clown Mask

Use inexpensive paper plates as the base for these easy-to-make masks. They can quickly be turned into people, animals, and imaginary creatures with a few supplies and a lot of imagination.

▶ Materials:

- inexpensive paper plates
- marking pens
- scissors
- glue (tacky glue works best)
- hole punch
- string - 12" (30.5 cm) - 2 pieces

Optional - "Found" objects to glue on for added interest (pipe cleaners, fabric, ribbon, foil, buttons, etc.).

Note: This mask is meant for supervised use. Unless the eye holes are quite large, the range of vision is somewhat limited. Don't wear it while walking about outside.

▶ Techniques to Use:

Curl, page 4
Slits, page 7

         Paper Crafts • EMC 723

Steps to Follow:

1. Hold the plate up to your face. Lick a finger and lightly tap the plate to mark the location of your eyes. Make an X with a pencil on each moist spot.

2. Lightly sketch in the clown's face including ears, hair, and "U" shaped nose.

3. Color the clown's face and hair.

4. Cut out sections of paper plate rim as shown, leaving "hair" and "collar." Fold ears forward.

5. Cut out eye holes. Cut along nose line and fold nose flap up.

6. Decorate collar.

7. Punch a hole on each side of face. Tie string to each hole.

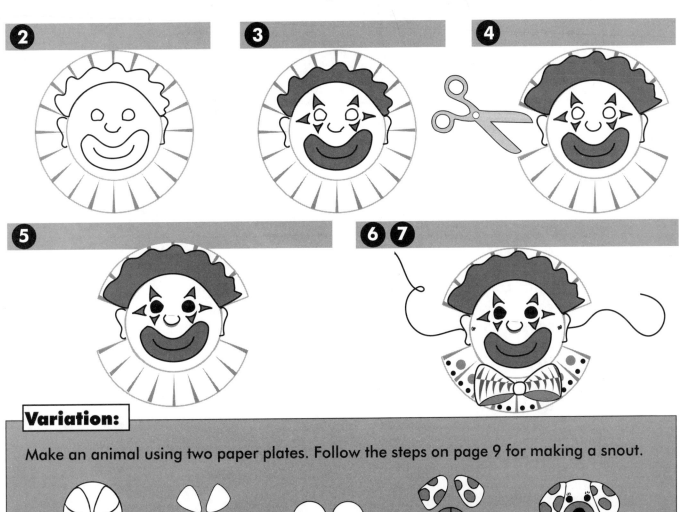

Variation:

Make an animal using two paper plates. Follow the steps on page 9 for making a snout.

1. Sketch. 2. Cut out. 3. Snout. 4. Color. 5. Glue.

Note: In step 4 put a thick layer of tacky glue around the edge of the cone and hold it in place for a minute while it sets. Or cut and fold slits (see page 9) and glue them in place.

3-D Paper Mask

These decorative masks begin with ordinary construction paper. Cuts, folds, fringe...all add to an outstanding final product.

► Materials:

- white construction paper - 9" x 12" (23 x 30.5 cm)
- construction paper - 4" x 6" (10 x 15 cm) for beak
- construction paper - 2"x 6" (5 x 15 cm) for each feather
- crayons or marking pens
- stapler
- scissors
- glue

Optional - "Found" objects to glue on for added interest (pipe cleaners, fabric, ribbon, foil, buttons, etc.).

► Techniques to Use:

Fringe, page 7
Symmetrical Fold, page 8
3-D Attachment, page 9

Paper Crafts • EMC 723

Steps to Follow:

1. Fold the 9" x 12" (23 x 30.5 cm) paper in half. Make cuts as shown.

2. Draw designs on mask using crayons or markers.

3. Overlap the paper slits and glue or staple.

4. Make a beak as shown. Glue to head.

5. Cut paper feathers as shown. Glue to head.

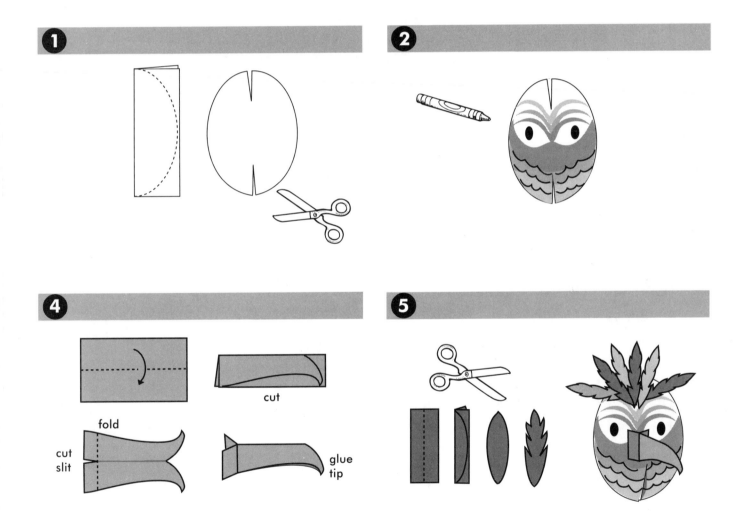

Ceremonial Mask

Ceremonial masks are worn or displayed in many cultures around the world. Share books containing pictures of various types of masks. Then set students loose to create their own versions.

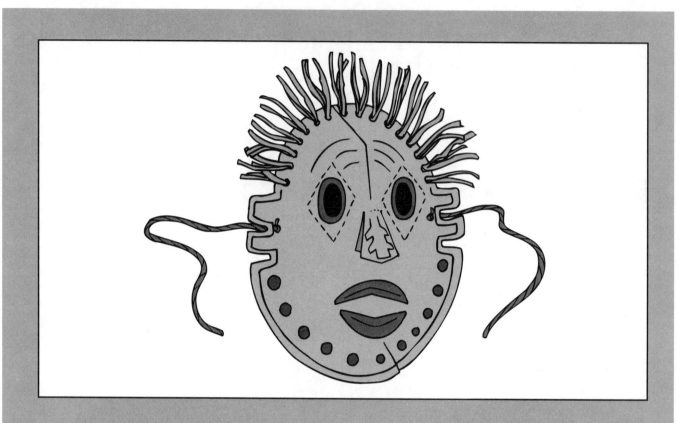

▶ Materials:
- construction paper - 9" x 12" (23 x 30.5 cm)
- scraps of paper - different sizes and colors
- raffia
- found objects
- scissors
- pencil
- glue
- hole punch

▶ Techniques to Use:
Rounding Corners, page 7
Symmetrical Pieces, page 8
3-D Attachment, page 9

Steps to follow:

1. Fold the 9" x 12" (23 x 30.5 cm) paper in half. Sketch the outline of the mask shape. Sketch and cut the nose while the paper is still folded.

2. Cut out the mask. Cut the eye holes.

3. Add details using marking pens.

4. To add a 3-dimensional look to the mask, make cuts as shown. Then overlap the paper and staple or glue.

5. Make a 3-dimensional mouth as shown. Glue to mask.

6. Hair can be added by punching holes and tying raffia to the mask.

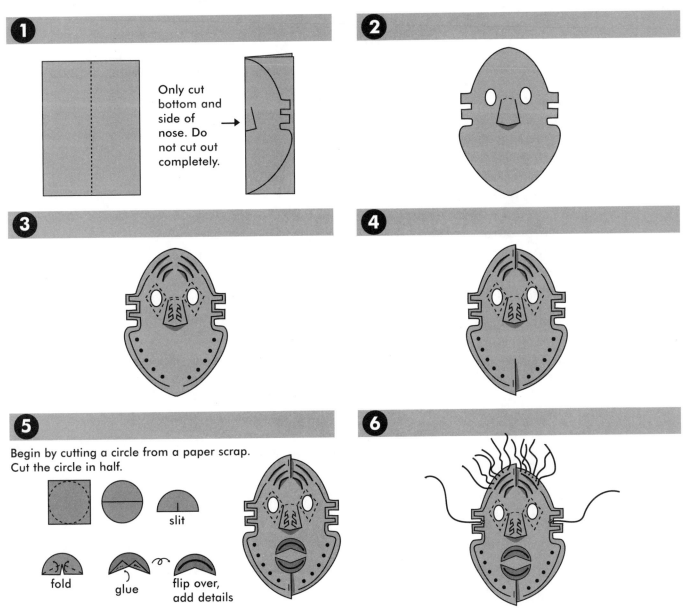

1

Only cut bottom and side of nose. Do not cut out completely.

2

3

4

5

Begin by cutting a circle from a paper scrap. Cut the circle in half.

slit

fold

glue

flip over, add details

6

3-D Forest

Free-standing plants can be made in many ways. This project asks students to try four different techniques as they build a wooded glen.

▶ Materials:

This list is for one of each type of tree per person.
- 2 pieces of green tagboard - 4" x 6" (10 x 15 cm)
- green construction paper
    - 3 - 4" x 6" (10 x 15 cm)
    - 1 - 6" (15 cm) square
    - 1 - 4" x 12" (10 x 30.5 cm)
- cardboard - approximately 12" x 18" (30.5 x 45.5 cm)
- crayons or marking pens
- scissors
- glue
- tape
- pencil

Optional - A supply of soil such as sand or fine potting bark to sprinkle on the cardboard for the forest floor.

Note: It will be easier for children to glue their trees to the cardboard if you provide "tacky" glue.

▶ Techniques to Use:

Roll, page 4
Slits, page 7
Symmetrical Pieces, page 8
3-D Attachment, page 9

Slotted Tree

1. Lightly sketch a tree on one piece of green tagboard. Cut it out. Lay the tree on the second piece of tag and trace around it. Cut it out.

2. Cut narrow slits to the middle of the trees as shown. Slip the trees together.

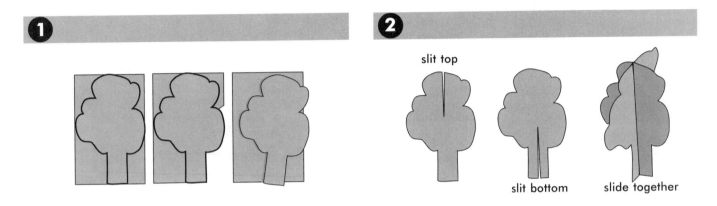

Three-Part Tree

1. Fold one piece of 4" x 6" (10 x 15 cm) green paper in half. Sketch half a tree on the paper starting at the top along the fold line. Cut out the tree.

2. Trace this same tree on the other two pieces of folded green paper. Cut them out.

3. Put glue along one half of each tree. Glue them together as shown.

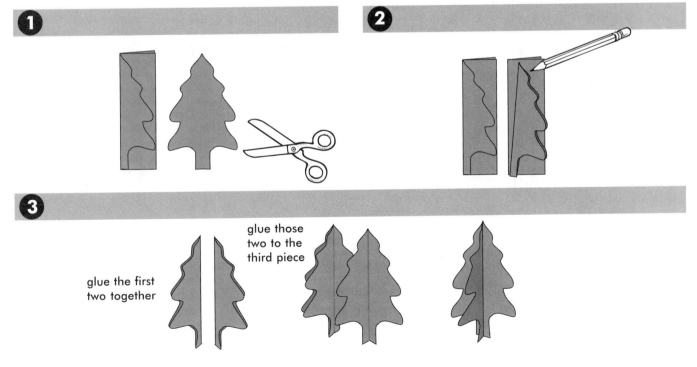

Rolled Tree

1. Loosely roll the 6" (15 cm) square to form a tube. Glue or tape the tube together.

2. Cut slits around one end. Make the slits to the middle of the tube.

3. Curl each piece of cut paper around a pencil to make the branches of the tree.

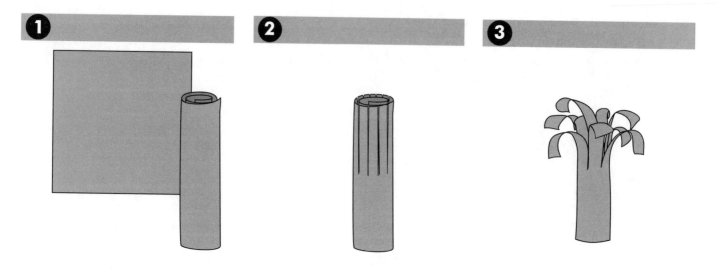

Folded Tree

1. Fold the 4" x 12" (10 x 30.5 cm) paper in half the long way.

2. Sketch a tree with a trunk on the paper.

3. Cut out the tree, making sure to leave part of the fold uncut.

4. Fold under a portion of the tree trunk on each side.

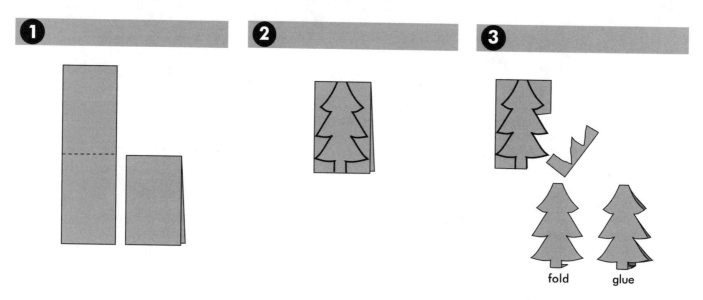

fold   glue

Assembling the Forest

1. Arrange the trees around your "forest." When you are happy with the arrangement, glue the trees to the cardboard. Add as many trees as you wish.

   To attach trees: Cut short slits around the base of the tree, fold to form tabs, and glue to the cardboard, or put a thick line of tacky glue along the bottom of the tree. Sit it in place and hold gently for a moment to let the glue begin to set.

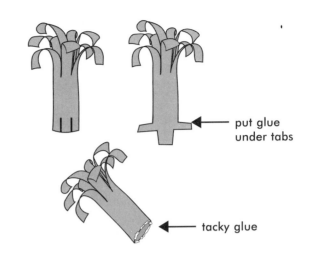

put glue under tabs

tacky glue

2. Spread glue over the cardboard. Sprinkle sand or bark on the wet glue to make the forest floor.

Variation:

Create other plants, some animals, or a person to add to your forest scene.

 Paper Crafts • EMC 723

Stuffed Paper Creations

Stuffing is a quick way to create large, colorful works of art. Begin with this "fishy" lesson, then move on to create rainforests, gardens, parades, etc., of "stuffed" creations.

▶ Materials:

- butcher paper - 18" x 24" (45.5 x 61 cm) - 2 sheets per child
- construction paper scraps - many colors
- marking pens or crayons
- scissors
- glue
- stapler

Optional - Found objects such as buttons, rickrack, ribbon, bottle caps, etc., to use for eyes and scales. Glitter to add sparkle to the fish.

Steps to Follow:

1. Sketch the outline of a fish on one sheet of butcher paper. Keep it simple. Fancy fins can be added from scraps later on.

2. Cut out two fish exactly the same shape and size.

3. Decorate both fish exactly the same.

4. Tear newspaper into strips to use as stuffing.

5. Staple or glue the tail fin sections together along the edge. Stuff the fins with newspaper. (If you use glue, let the fish dry before you try to stuff it.)

6. Staple or glue the sides of the fish and stuff the body with newspaper.

7. Staple or glue around the mouth area to close off the fish.

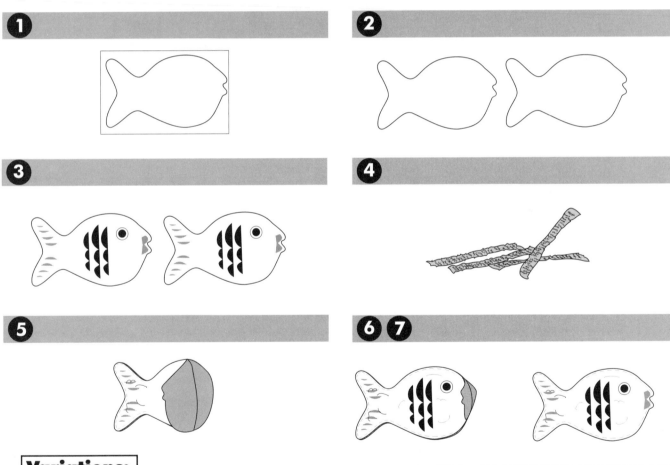

Variations:

Punch holes around the outside edge of the fish. Lace it together using yarn.

Cut a fish from felt. Sew it together with a large plastic needle and yarn.

Make a Slinky Snake

This "hiss-terical" snake is a great favorite of children of all ages.

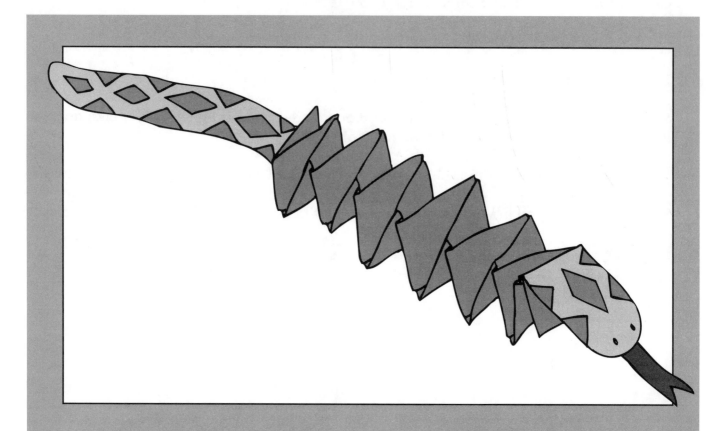

▶ **Materials:**
- green paper strips - 1" x 18" (2.5 x 45.5 cm) - 2 per snake
- yellow paper strip - 1" x 12" (2.5 x 30.5 cm)
- scrap of red paper at least 2" (5 cm) long
- scissors
- glue
- crayons
- ruler

▶ **Techniques to Use:**
Jacob's Ladder, page 6
3-D Attachment, page 9

Steps to Follow:

1. Make a Jacob's Ladder (page 6) with the two green strips.

2. Cut 3" (7.5 cm) off the yellow strip. Draw the snake's head. Cut it out.

3. Draw a tail on the rest of the strip. Draw scales on the tail. Cut it out.

4. Cut a forked tongue out of the red scrap.

5. Glue the parts together.

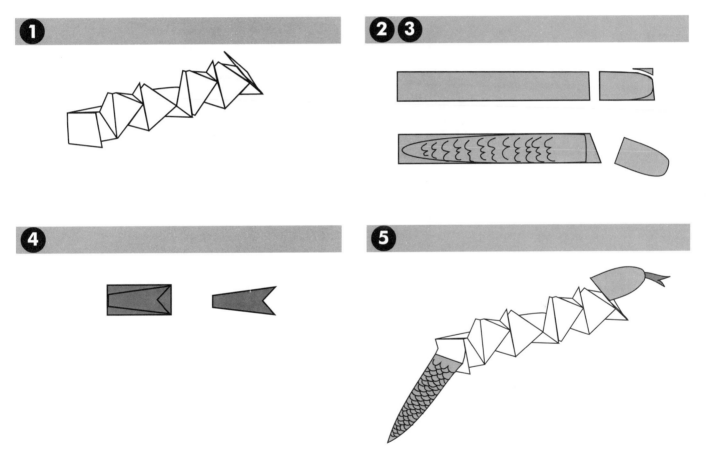

Variation:

Make a "snapping" snake's head out of a 6" (15 cm) square of paper following these steps:

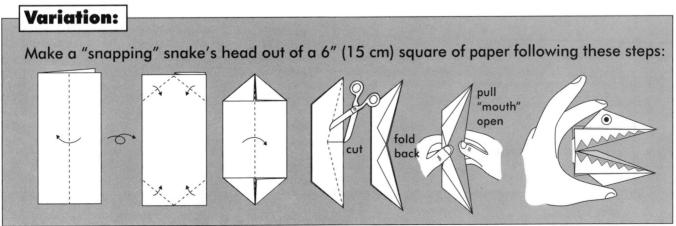

cut

fold back

pull "mouth" open

Cross-Legged Critters

Cross-legged critters are fun to make. The size can be varied by using different sized squares. The pocket formed in the center can be filled with information about the "critter" or treats for a special occasion.

▶ Materials:

Cross-Legged Ball Player
- blue construction paper
  - 9" (23 cm) square - body
- tan construction paper
  (or other skin color)
  - 3" (7.5 cm) square - head
  - 1" (2.5 cm) square - hands
- red construction paper
  - 3" square (7.5 cm) - cap
- scissors
- glue
- stapler
- crayons

Cross-Legged Turkey
- brown construction paper
  - 9" (23 cm) square - body
  - 3" (7.5 cm) square - wings
- orange construction paper
  - 3 -3" (7.5 cm) squares- feathers
- red construction paper
  - 2" x 3" (5 x 7.5 cm) - head
- scissors
- glue
- stapler
- crayons

▶ Techniques to Use:
Rounding Corners, page 7

Begin with the 9" (23 cm) square of construction paper.

Follow these steps:

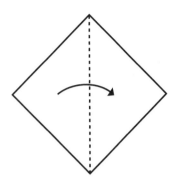

a.
fold in half, corner to
corner, then re-open

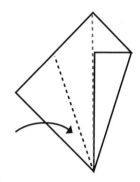

b.
fold in to center line

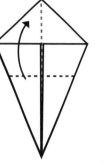

c.
fold narrow point
up to top point

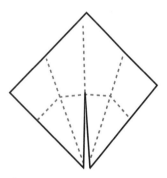

d.
Open the paper. Cut
up the center line.
Stop in the middle.

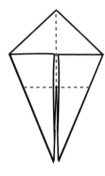

e.
Re-fold the paper.
Cross the legs.

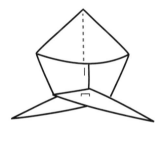

f.
Staple foot.
Staple pocket.
(pull out to staple)

       Paper Crafts • EMC 723

Body

Make the basic cross-legged critter shape with the big blue square.

body

Head

1. Round off the corners of the large tan square to make the head.

head

2. Round off the corners of the red paper to make the cap. Fold the circle in half.

cap

3. Glue the cap on the head like a baseball cap. The brim turns up.

4. Use crayons to draw eyes, nose, and mouth. Draw in hair peeking out from under the cap.

Body Parts

hands

1. Round the corners of the small tan square to make the hands. Glue the circle to the body. Add fingers with crayon if you wish.

2. Use a black crayon to draw on the arm lines.

3. Round off the tips of the feet. Draw shoelaces.

Optional - Add other details such as a team insignia on the cap or a bat and ball in the ball player's hands.

Variation:

Use the same basic shape to create another person.

 Paper Crafts • EMC 723

Body

Make the basic cross-legged critter shape with the big brown square.

body

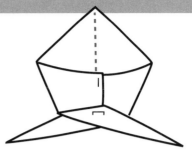

Feathers

1. Fold each piece of orange paper in half and cut along the fold line.

2. Cut each piece to a point.

3. Glue the feathers on the back of the turkey's body.

feathers

1.   2.

3.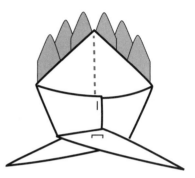

Head

1. Make the head by rounding the corners of the red paper to form an oval. Cut a slit as shown.

2. Draw an eye with a black crayon. Turn the head over and draw the other eye.

3. Make a beak using an orange scrap left from the feathers.

4. Cut scallops along the edge of the head below the beak to make the turkey's wattle.

5. Slip the turkey's head on the front of the turkey's body.

head

   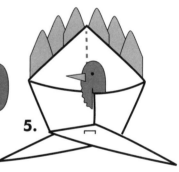

1.   2.   3.   4.   5.

Wings

1. Round the corners of the small brown square. Fold it in half.

2. Open and cut on the fold.

3. Glue the wings to the turkey's body.

wings

1.

2.

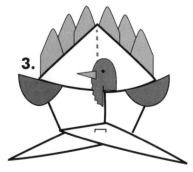
3.

                                       Paper Crafts • EMC 723

3-D Bouquet

Use the technique of scoring paper and folding to create a charming three-dimensional bouquet of flowers. Make all tulips, all daisies, or a combination of both. The bouquet will look best if you have an odd number of flowers.

▶ **Materials**
- construction paper -
  12" x 18" (30.5 x 45.5 cm)
  for background
- construction paper -
  6" x 9" (15 x 23 cm) for vase
- scissors
- glue
- pencil

Daisy:
- yellow or white construction paper
  1" x 2" (2.5 x 5 cm) - daisy petals
- black construction paper
  1" x 2" (2.5 x 5 cm) - daisy center
- green construction paper
  2" x 3" (5 x 7.5 cm) - daisy leaves
  1/2" x 12" (1 x 30.5cm) - flower
  stems (cut to fit flower need)

Tulip:
- assorted colors of construction paper
  3" x 3" (7.5 x 7.5 cm) - outer petals
  1 1/2" x 3" (4 x 7.5 cm) - inside petal
- green construction paper
  1" x 12" (2.5 x 30.5 cm) - tulip leaves
  1/2" x 12" (1 x 30.5cm) - flower
  stems (cut to fit flower need)

▶ **Techniques to Use:**
Scoring, page 6
Rounding Corners, page 7
Symmetrical Pieces, page 8

 Paper Crafts • EMC 723

Steps to Follow:

If children have difficulty scoring with scissors, have them use a paper clip that has been opened up.

Vase

1. Fold the 6" x 9" (15 x 23 cm) paper in half.

2. Cut a vase freehand starting at the fold, or lightly sketch in the vase shape and then cut it out.

3. Score the vase near the sides. Fold along your score line. Fold the outside edges back and the center fold forward to make the vase 3-dimensional.

4. Glue the vase about 1/4 of the way up the background paper.

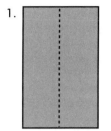
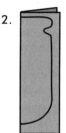
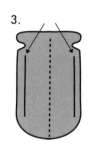

Daisy

1. Fold each 1" x 2" (2.5 x 5 cm) paper in half the long way. Cut out the daisy petals.

2. Fold the black construction paper in half. Round the corners to make a circle.

3. Glue the petals around one circle. Glue the other circle on top of the petals.

4. Fold the green 2" x 3" paper in half. Cut out a leaf.

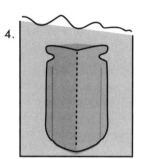

Tulip

1. Fold the 1 1/2" x 3" paper in half lengthwise. Cut the inside petal.

2. Fold the 3" square in half. Cut the outside petals. Score the outside petals near the edge. Fold along the score line.

3. Cut the 1" x 12" (2.5 x 30.5 cm) green strips into leaves. Score them the long way.

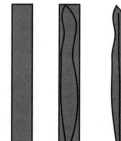

77

Assemble the Bouquet

1. Place stems in the vase. Cut the stems different lengths. Place the flowers and leaves on the stems. Move the pieces around until you find an arrangement you like.

2. Glue the pieces down.
   a. Glue the stems first. Put glue on both ends of the stem. Don't place the stem flat against the paper. Glue it loosely to give the stem a 3-D look.

   b. Glue the flowers on the stems.

glue down underneath scored edge

   c. Glue on the leaves.

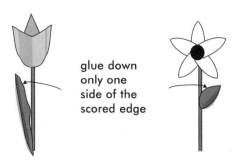

glue down only one side of the scored edge

Note: Challenge children to create their own homes in 3-dimensional form from flat paper. Encourage them to include items such as plants, curtains, etc.

Challenge

_____'s Home

Build a model of your house using paper and the techniques you have learned. Add special details such as curtains, plants, garage, etc.

List your materials here:

_____	_____
_____	_____
_____	_____
_____	_____
_____	

Write the steps you followed here:

1. _____

2. _____

3. _____

4. _____

5. _____

6. _____

Use the back of this page if you need more space.
Put this form with your finished project.

 Paper Crafts • EMC 723

Challenge
Make a Diorama

Build a diorama that tells a story. It must contain at least three of these:
- a person
- one or more plants
- one or more animals
- some sort of dwelling
- something flying in the sky

Plan your diorama scene here. Make a sketch of how you want it to look.

List the materials you will need:

_____   _____

_____   _____

_____   _____

_____   _____

_____   _____